The Guinea Pig ABC

The

Guinea Pig ABC
by Kate Duke

E. P. DUTTON   NEW YORK

Published in the United States by E. P. Dutton,
2 Park Avenue, New York, N.Y. 10016

Editor: Ann Durell   Designer: Claire Counihan

Printed in Hong Kong by South China Printing Co.

10 9 8 7 6 5

Library of Congress Cataloging in Publication Data

Duke, Kate.
    The guinea pig ABC.

    Summary: Each letter of the alphabet is illustrated
by a word which applies to pictured guinea pigs.
    [1. Alphabet.   2. Guinea pigs]   I. Title.
PZ7.D886Gu   1983   [E]   83-1410
ISBN 0-525-44058-5

Awake

Bouncy

Clean

Dirty

Empty

Ferocious

Greedy

High

Itchy

Juicy

Kind

Loud

Mean

Neat

Open

Prickly

Quiet

Rich

Slippery

Timid

Upside-down

Vain

Wobbly

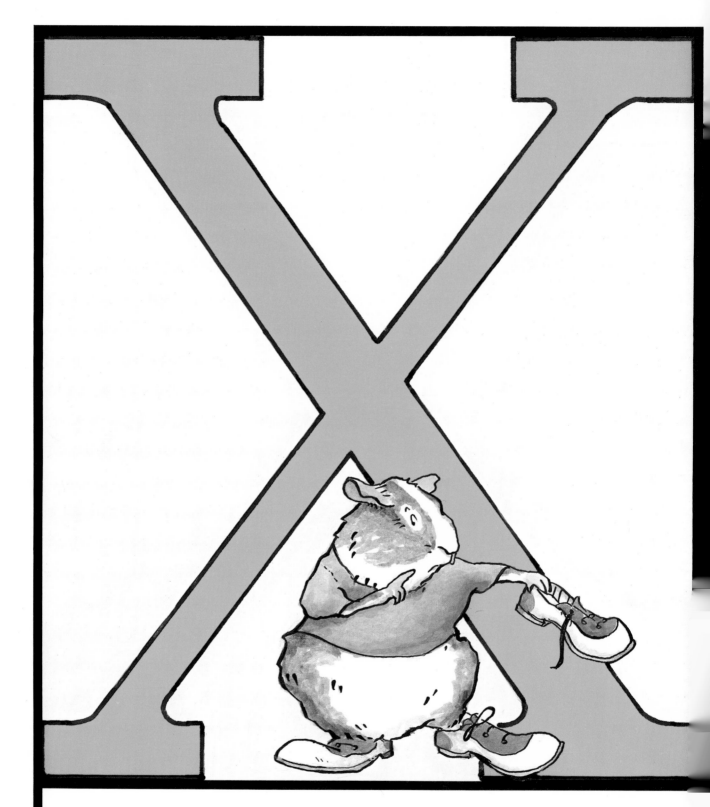

eXtra

Young

Zzzzzzzzz